Coffee, Dreams, and Tears

by

Jessica Rose

RoseDog Books

PITTSBURGH, PENNSYLVANIA 15238

RoseDog Books
585 Alpha Drive, Suite 103
Pittsburgh, PA 15238
Visit our website at *www.rosedogbookstore.com*

ISBN: 979-8-89211-230-7
eISBN: 979-8-89211-728-9

Introduction

This collection of poems is dear to my heart, revealing my struggles and hurt, and my hope and help that I've encountered in my years. I will discuss matters that alot do not, however it is OK. It's part of life. And we are Diving to the Deep.

If you are described by the world as an "outcast", a felon, drug addict or alcoholic, someone who stuggles with mental health, trauma, or fear, then I am one of you and I PROMISE you, there is hope. So what if we're different, guess what!?! EVERYONE is different. That is the beauty of it, that we are all unique and have our own special gifts and qwirks.

Speaking of life, we will touch on Domestic Violence Awareness, Addiction and Recovery, the Prison world, and hope in the now. I hope that reading these will give my readers insight to difficult situations, that they may not have fully understood otherwise.

Happy reading! You guys rock!

Your Friend,

Jessi

Coffee Dreams and Tears   1/31/2017

Always in a hurry to get the kids to school,

She can't be late, this is works number one rule.

She dips and dodges, through traffic she steers,

She will make it today on coffee, dreams, and tears.

Cooking supper, homework, bath-time, and reading,

That she can meet all their needs is all she is pleading.

That their Mama didn't have enough time for them is one of her biggest
fears,

So she gets little sleep while getting by on coffee, dreams, and tears.

She only wants to be the best role model she can,

Trying to show the kids that everything fits into her plan.

Trying to be strong, Godly, and independent for it is she that her children
mirrors,

She puts on her best face and struggles to succeed through coffee, dreams,
and tears.

Paying bills, grocery shopping, and making it to their games,

Being there for them to talk to and know their friends' names.

Same routine, same struggles for countless years,

But she remains strong through coffee, dreams, and tears.

When things become too much, she'll break down and cry while she's alone,

She's practiced this for years, where her feeling of defeat will not be shown.

She pulls herself together and prays while slowly her mind clears,

She can do it, it's just another day with coffee, dreams, and tears.

Car problems, fund raisers, field trips, and the report card,

On some weeks more than others, keeping up is very hard.

Church events, work deadlines, and the date things need to be paid nears,

She tries to stay on top of the chaos through coffee, dreams, and tears.

Graduations, proms, first dates, and senior night,

Taking her daughter shopping for the dress that fits just right.

I love you Mom, I couldn't have done it without you is what she hears,

She knows it was worth all the coffee, dreams, and tears.

She teaches them to be leaders, that they can do anything,

To have courage that their dreams can fly on an eagles wing.

One day when her schedule finally clears,

She will thank God for having made it through, with coffee, dreams, and tears.

Understanding

10/4/2018

As I sit here in prison I could be ashamed, mad, fearful, or hurt,

I let everyone down again, same conviction, makes me feel like dirt.

But I will not sit here and mope, I want absolutely no pity or grief,

For my prison sentence was sent to me, again not for pain, but for relief.

I was not strong enough to tackle the demons I had on my own,

I had to be pulled away, set down, once again, I had to really be shown.

God knew I needed help and that He had to find a way to open my eyes,

My addiction, my relationship, my life out of control, and I was too blind to realize.

He teaches me so much while im here and I remain thankful for every day,

Honestly right now, I'm so lost in life, that I would rather it this way.

I know too well how things go here, its even comfortable and not scary,

On the outside I had too much freedom, it was almost twice it was me they had to bury.

You are only able to find the way, when you come to reality that you are lost,

To find God and my purpose again, this line had to shamefully be crossed.

Recovered

5/1/2019

When I got here I was broken, felt worthless, and didn't know how to feel,

What I got from recovery and rehab was a sobriety that was very real.

I had to face my demons, feel my emotions, and learn how to do whats right,

Without drinking I had no option but to go through the step and choose the path that was bright.

It was hard at first being in so much darkness, from the world I wanted to hide,

Little did I know that in the end id be making the choice to stay sober and wanting to confide.

I am able to talk about what ive been through, trust in my support, and finally feel once again,

This program has taught me how to succeed, for once I have the tools to win.

We're Not Gunna Take It   10/4/2016

There's been too many victims with scars that will never heal,

You need to know you are not alone, there are so many who have felt what you feel.

Being so many different strains and levels of abuse, not one being more important than the other,

Too many times by boyfriends, girlfriends, uncles, father, mother, sister, or brother.

I want you to know and remember that not one of you deserved what has happened to you,

The victims who have spoken about and shared their pain and torture are unfortunately very few.

Today is the day to bring this memory to the surface, to rid yourself from the pain,

You have nothing to lose, it's time to change, you have everything to gain!

He or she cannot hurt you anymore, you have the choice to never go back,

You can rid yourself of all the pain, anger, and guilt, TODAY you can get your life back on track.

Sexual, physical, financial, mental, and emotional, not one of these can you not overcome,

You can no longer let this burden you!, take back control of your life!, the damage has already been done.

You are worthy of rest, comfort, and hope for your future NO longer letting this dominate,

Let's be able to help each other, overcome this pain, share together, communicate.

Wouldn't you want to help those the same as you? Wouldn't you take away their pain?

Everyone you love wants to help you too, from the hurt just refrain!

You can be a new person today, never again who you used to be,

Give it up, let it hurt you no more, from these chains you can be set free!

You are beautiful inside and out and it's time to let it show!

Step over the hurt, leave it behind, while your confidence begins to grow.

There is a safe place where you cannot be harmed, in the arms of Jesus Christ,

He will protect you and never leave you if you believe that for you, He was sacrificed.

He can take away the hurt, the pain, and the memories and forgive your old life of sin,

You can renew yourself and live a comfortable life if you simply open your heart and ask Him in.

For Domestic Violence Seminar   Logan Correctional Center 2016

With Pain Comes Strength

11/6/2016

This road you're traveling down is one to test your strength,

It will break you, shape you, teach you wisdom, taking you to every length.

I want you to know how strong you are already, to have made it this far,

I'm sure in your head is a struggle, battle, the hardest, most ultimate war.

It would be easy to be mad, to give up, to freak the hell out,

But what you're doing, nearing to God, is the way you need no doubt.

You should be proud of yourself, not everyone can stand strong like you've already done,

You're doin a great job in doing what you need for you daughter and son.

Though some days are harder than others, you've already proven that you can overcome,

Holding yourself together, being responsible for the kids, you're showing them where Mom comes from.

Staying solid, never falling, proving yourself a true daughter of The Lord,

Girl you should be proud, you're doin a great job, by God you are fully adored.

Ladies I am here today so that maybe you won't make the same mistake I did,

I never wanted to speak up because the abuse had made me scared and timid.

But not saying anything was the worst thing I could have done,

For this was no game, no joking matter, and most deffinately, not fun.

For too long victims keep getting abused for the fact they are scared to say anything,

The limit to what the abuser will do can't be taken light, DEATH to you this could bring!

All forms of abuse need to be stopped, someone stand against the violence!

Not just for your case but for others too, we have to end the silence!

No one deserves to be abused, be the one who's not afraid to say it loud!

Help someone put an end to the torture, lets make a change and stand up proud!

If it happens once, it WILL happen again, it's never your fault, for this there's no excuse!

You're beautiful and deserve better, NO one should have to live in a life of abuse!

Listen to the unspoken word, let the bruises, scraped up knees, black eyes find a voice,

To not let it keep happening we have to not be afraid to make a crucial choice.

For Domestic Violence Seminar   Logan Correctional Center   2016

Don't Come To Prison 1/12/2019

Don't forget how lucky you are to be able to touch the one you love,

Or how safe and comfortable you are in the arms of the man you dream of.

Never take for granted being able to talk to them and daily hear their voice,

When your addiction gets the best of you remember you do have a choice.

Not having to miss looking in their eyes or the feeling of their hair,

You will never have to need or want because what you want will be right there.

The people you love cant touch you or feel your embrace around them,

You feel always a need, an aloneness, fullness can only come from her or him.

I dont think you unaware people understand how deep is this longing,

You try not to think or feel but the inevitable is only prolonging.

Being away from the ones you love leaves an emptiness inside your heart,

Like its been pierced by a honing arrow, or poisoned by a dart.

Which Way 2/15/2017

At the lowest point of my life, I have never seen so much light,

Though the place is still dark, I finally have hope to make things right.

I very easily could feel abandoned, alone, guilt, and hate,

But with God in my life i'm deciding to choose a different fate.

I realize now that God isn't punishing me, but giving me a second chance,

I am very lucky, no very fortunate, to be in this circumstance.

In these walls lives hostility, ignorance, ruthlessness, and diversity,

It's terrible here but in my life I have never felt so free.

I am beginning my walk and learning that on God I can fully rely,

When everyone in the world has let me down, God will always hear my cry.

It is a process to live obediently and to fully take in what God is trying to say,

For me to love others and get them to believe in Him is what He hopes for each day.

He wants to give us the gift of salvation and love if we would only accept,

This very drawn out guideline of how life should be, is actually a simple concept.

Choosing to spend my time in daily devotionals, church, retreats, and Bible class,

I am learning how to live right instead of cheat, lie, steal, and harass.

In here its easy to do wrong, to learn to be a better criminal than I was,

But I have chosen to not be part of this world, of the flesh, but to do what Jesus does.

You've been such an inspiration to many, your smile you can can make our day,

You are strong, determined, and ambitious, I know you'll be good, come what may.

While being here you completely made yourself new, being so much more knowledgable than you used to be,

You've accomadated a new mind-set, a beautiful attitude, and the realization that God is the key.

You should be proud of yourself, the better woman you are from here on out,

You will accomplish so many things and help many people, I know without a doubt.

You are encouraging, up-lifting, and full of wisdom and understanding,

Follow your heart, use your talents, the urge to help others for you is demanding.

Don't be nervous, you got this, you've completed everything you need,

You are changed, have God on your side, and now able to fulfill any deed.

Have faith upon leaving that this time you will live among abundant joy,

For now, your emotions, wrong doings, and anger, with the devil will not be able to toy.

Congratulations girl, you made it through this prison sentence that is much like hell,

You will be a success story, with an amazing testimony, for yourself doing very well.

Love ya girl

God Bless You

Why Care When They Don't

1/17/2017

Sometimes I wonder if I even know what i'm doing,

In my head there are so many ideas, good and bad that are brewing.

Sometimes I feel like I'm really not sure of anything,

All I have control of is to the table what I can bring.

I have alot of relationships but I used to have more,

All the sudden I don't exist, since I've walked through this door.

I realize I only need a few people, but are those relationships even right?

In here you tend to see people in a whole different light.

Only having a few people, who still care about me at all,

People wonder why I never let my guard down and continue to have my wall.

I won't let people get to me when I know most don't really care,

The idea of being hurt, the feeling of being unwanted i'm too tired to bare.

Grandma and Papa - 50th Anniversary   8/21/2016

Its been fifty years since you came together as one,

That special day can be replaced by none.

You've spent life together, creating all the memories you have now,

Still embedded in you, every commitment, every vow.

Through sickness and health, happiness and pain, the ups and downs,

You've been there for each other through everything, rarely having worn the frowns.

Many don't get the chance to witness their celebrating the anniversary of 50 years,

So feel happy, honored, excited as your once in a lifetime celebration nears! :)

Raise your heads up high and be proud of the honor you will recieve,

For obviously love, respect, loyalty, and happiness is in all that you believe.

Congratulations on this incredible day you will never forget,

Taking you back and being ever thankful for that day you first met.

A Good Rhyme or Reason 10/20/2016

I'm finally starting to believe that all my dreams are coming true,

Through God is the only way I have managed to make it through.

With His Grace, Guidance, and Will, I am finally seeing the light,

My life for once is looking great, in the eye of my sight.

Coming to prison has saved me from the road to death I was headed down,

Treatment from Westcare gives me understanding, hope, realization, and knowledge of the addiction I need to drown.

I am blessed with three beautiful healthy girls,

All with gorgeous blue eyes, one with straight hair, two with curls.

They're my life and my reason for changes i'm making,

When I get out I have a job that I love that is still mine for the taking.

Finally found a man who treats me better than I could ever dream of,

Didn't know this was possible this overwhelming, breathtaking kind of love.

It sounds pretty good the way my life is now, from how it used to be,

Let me go back and take you to my past so what I hide you can see.

I spent my childhood alone, having no sister or brother,

Have two sisters from my dad whom I still havn't met, for they have a different mother.

It was only me and my mom growing up, she didn't want dad around because of the alcohol,

I totally understand being older now and I have the same disease that I have no control over alcohol at all.

Since I was born i've had a birthmark that kept me going to the hospital at least twice a year,

MRI's CT scans, student doctors, the irregular, enlarged blood vessels beneath it was their biggest fear.

Can you imagine a strong, scared mom, not fully understanding in a chair rocking me to sleep every night,

Her only baby, with something wrong, but the depth of it they still had to find out, meanwhile praying everything would turn out alright.

Through school I was restricted to one sport at a time for if I got too worn down it would make me very sick,

Although in some ways I am grateful for my birthmark for it made me appreciative, humble, and my skin very thick.

During my senior year, I took my general classes for the study of cosmetology because I like to cut hair,

After graduating and proceeding into the program, I realized doing nails and being around women all day, the interest was not there.

So I dropped out, now being a "legal adult" and having all the time in the world, I began my own way to live,

Drinking all day every day, doing all drugs, I've done some things that I, myself can't even forgive.

This lead me in and out of jail in six different counties, moving out of three towns because the cops knew me so well,

Bail money, court, tickets, impounded belongings, jail about twenty times, my life was going to hell.

When moving to the first town I met the man who eventually became my husband,

We were partners in crime, selling pot, having control, drugs, and money, my best friend he has always been.

We have done many criminal acts, loving the adrenaline, suspense, and living the life to rebel,

This is the "good life", the fun we had before off the mountain we fell.

We tried for our first kid for four years, before having our daughter, after having her things were never the same,

Then the mental abuse, hatred, insecurities, sobriety, and the first suicide attempt came.

After getting home from work and taking a shower, he decided he no longer wanted to be around,

He went to the bedroom when our baby was three months old and elevated himself by his neck above the ground.

I went back there in time and took the belt from around his neck, and made sure he was still alive,

This was the point when insanity, trauma, guilt, confusion, and realization put my brain in over-drive.

I was a mess trying to raise my first baby, trying to figure out the question of what to do,

Shortly after breaking up and back together, I needed a new start in Salem that was completely brand new.

I enrolled in college at Kaskaskia finally knowing what I loved to do,

I graduated in May, 2014 from Automotive Tech, for my passion to be a mechanic was true.

I had my second daughter and married the man that I spent years with before, hoping things would change,

But the anxiety, hatred, anger, addiction, unhealthy relationship, and drugs still had a very wide range.

We could no longer be together, for we fought too much and grew apart,

It was finally time to face the reality that things would never be how they were at the start.

Still being friends and the father of my girls, I wanted to help him how I could,

Knowing the cops were after him, I took him to our home town, and left him where I thought I should.

Long story short I was getting a call from the hospital saying he was in critical condition,

Trying to commit suicide for the third time, this was starting to become a horrible tradition.

Only by the grace of God not lettin him end it this way did he breathe without the tube he had been on,

Taking forty phenobarbatol to stop his heart, only by God could this line he drew be withdrawn.

So here I am seven months pregnant, still working, dealing with doctors, kids, and fines,

With way too much stress and anxiety, feeling like i'm walking through a field of mines.

After having my third baby Nya, the father of my youngest moved in with my kids and me.

Such a great dad, encouraging, up-lifting, supportive, and treating me like a queen.

When I got sentenced to prison on my case, it seemed horrible at the time,

But with being in and out of the psych ward and jail, I can see everything has a reason and rhyme.

Being here at Logan, even though I hate to admit, has brought much realization to my mind,

Realization of my skills, talents, and God-given gifts are what i've come to finally utilize and find.

Getting treatment for the addiction I never wanted to admit is deffinately what I needed,

Learning my behaviors, addiction, myself and triggers, to the correct way of thinking it had leaded.

Growing up in church i've always known God, but i've never fully understood the way of living,

Reading daily devotionals, praying, and making stronger our relationship, I realize that God's about helping and giving.

To treat others even better than ourselves, and to always be inspirational, courteous, and kind,

This new way of living, by His Will, if i'd have never came to prison, I wouldn't have been able to find.

I am fortunate that God chose to keep me alive and give me a chance, yet again,

Showing me how to do right this time and what all I was missing in my life
of sin.

I'm more than blessed to go home to my daughters, my job, the man of my
dreams and more,

Being appreciative, humble, changed, and renewed I can't wait to see what
God has in store.

Real Shit

1/8/17

Some days in the joint are alot harder than others,

We all locked up feel the same hurt, brothers, sisters, mothers.

And you're never gettin out has turned into one of your deepest fears,

The longing that you have inside that you've never needed so much,

The desperate need of love and ever steady wanting to feel someones touch.

If youve been here, you felt this, then you already know,

When it comes down to it, in the end you gotta reap what you sow.

Our sentence seems to take forever, no matter how long we actually face,

Surrounded by bitches, petty ass drama, all we really want's some fucking space.

Not very much can make it any better, it still sucks beyond belief,

If they do open the gate, say your time is up, you can never understand the relief

The path i've known has always been dark,

Simple rules, try all drugs, don't be a nark.

It's easy to go down all the wrong roads,

Criminal conduct, addiction, trouble by the loads.

But where the difficulty is is trying to turn this around,

The game is realizing how to change before buried underground.

Too many never get second chances, one bad move and they're gone,

Some choose to party all night, but never wake up for the dawn.

Luckily i've had the opportunity to recieve many chances,

I now have the suggestion to act apporpriately in future circumstances.

Since my prison sentence, I asked for help and admitted my flaws,

I am now seeking guidance, and my life has a real cause.

Liking Me

Finally, do you believe it? I can stand up tall,

I know quite a ways to go, but its OK I don't know it all.

Day by day i'm growing, learning, and believing in myself,

I'm realizing what is important in life is not drugs, fame, or wealth.

Becoming who I really am is not something I thought I needed to do,

Now I realize I wasn't myself and my thinking was not at all true.

I had to learn to be me, get to know myself again,

What I liked, what are my wants, who I was when my life began.

I'm finally becoming a person who I'm not ashamed to be,

I'm learning to be a woman of dignity, and now that defines me.

Trying to Explain the Unexplainable

Everytime he walks in the room, you go weak in the
knees, your breath becomes short, you get butterflies,
in your stomach, you are in love.

Everytime you kiss him, it seems as if the world stops,
turning, you see no one except you and him, you wish
you could stop time, you are in love.

Everytime you hold him, you never want to let go, you
want to feel every heartbeat, you want it to last
forever, you are in love.

Everytime you miss him, you can't think of anything
except him, you wish over and over that you could be
there with him, you are in love.

Everytime you talk to him, the little things he says makes
your day, you never want to stop talking, you wake up
everyday in hope of talking to him, you are in love.

Everytime you hear his name, you feel all tingly inside,
you hope you get to see him soon, you instantly miss
him, you are in love.

Everytime you love him, you sit here trying to explain
what you cannot but you know he understands
exactly what you mean... that is love.

Always and Forever

The Quiet One

12/28/2016

There are good days and there are bad,

Most days are better when I don't have to discuss my dad.

Many things of my childhood led me to be the way I am,

I feel like I have all the weight and responsibility like i'm holding a dam.

I struggle with trust issues, over-responsibility, and abandonment,

For someone to come into my life and stay would be heaven sent.

Maybe someday I will trust someone, opening up and trusting all the way,

Until I can get past this and believe in someone, little will I say.

Getting There

12/15/2016

Step one, step two, step three, step four,

so many revelations have come knocking at my door.

I came to this group blind and extremely unknowing,

Now the understanding and wisdom is steady ever-flowing.

I didn't realize how lost I was till I actually became found,

I finally feel like i'm walking on the path of solid ground.

In The Night

2/20/2019

When did my life come to this where I can't sleep without a pill,

These damn thoughts colliding in my head they seem to never get their fill.

My thoughts are scary, demented, when did I become this dark,

The fear and pain, me being scared, its all finding ways to leave their mark.

I'm not the same as I used to be, I'm not that happy girl anymore,

I feel ripped apart and bleeding, my head apart is tore.

Will there ever be an end, will I ever learn to not be afraid?

My demons continue to haunt me from company I kept and choices I made.

The Unaware

12/6/2016

These prison walls sure open your eyes to whats real,

It's been so long since I've thought, soaked in how I feel.

It ain't no joke, there is no doubt about that,

Been so long since I've been in my head and just sat.

We all need slowed down to open back up our eyes,

Unaware, disturbed, we're livin like zombies and don't even realize.

Numb to feeling, life, and who we used to once be,

Though I'm locked up, I'm finally starting to be free.

We don't realize how much we lose ourselves till we step back and take a look,

Make known our talents, be who we are, hell, sit down and read a book.